NEGOTIATING

POWERFUL AND EFFECTIVE STRATEGIES TO IMPROVE YOUR NEGOTIATION SKILLS AND SECURE THE BEST DEALS FOR YOU

Copyright © Richard Wall 2017
All Rights Reserved.

Table of Contents

Introduction 7

Why You Need to Build Upon Your Negotiation Skills 12

Commonly Used Negotiation Styles 20

Planning a Negotiation Session 36

How to Establish Rapport with Someone Quickly 43

How to Read People 61

How to Identify the Needs of Your Counterpart 67

The Big Open 72

Managing Manipulation 77

The Use of Leverage 90

The Closer 97

How to Secure a Pay Raise 101

Quick Negotiation Strategies 107

Negotiation Case Studies 113

Negotiating By Phone or Email 122

Negotiation Checklist 128

Conclusion 133

Introduction

It is next to impossible these days for anyone to truly get everything one wants. Negotiations are needed when dealing with people just to get somewhere.

The fact is that everyone prefers discussions that are fair and understandable. They want to establish strong relationships that are not hard to maintain or follow.

Negotiations are critical as they create a sensible compromise between two or more sides. These often involve two sides that have different views or ideas over what they want to get out of their lives or efforts.

Sometimes such discussions entail trying to move ahead. You might try to negotiate your way into something that is a little more advantageous to you than it is to the other party. But even this could involve plenty of cunning and strategy if used well enough.

In other instances, it all involves just trying to keep the damage in a situation from being worse. It is about keeping people happy while establishing longer relationships that made on trust and comfort towards one another.

Negotiations take place for many reasons. Sometimes they involve business partnerships or transactions. They might even involve more personal things. You might negotiate a plan to get a better salary, for instance.

When proper discussions take place, it becomes easier for all sides to get along and see the needs each person has. The parties can then hammer out details on an agreement that ensures each side gets as close to what one wants as possible. There is always the chance that you might influence the discussion to go in your favor too although you would have to be extremely careful when trying to make that happen.

It is true that each side will not get everything that they want. But with enough negotiating, it becomes easier for those sides to at least get what they want in various ways or to keep a situation in check.

You must use proper skills to improve upon how much you can get out of a discussion. Using the right efforts will help you get a chat to move smoothly and in a way where all parties involved will appreciate the work you are doing. Even more importantly, there is a potential that you might produce a better plan for work.

But to make it work, you have to get along with everyone you are talking with. You have to establish rapport and understand the needs others hold. Getting on the same page as others might sound tough to do but when handled right it can make a true impact on your work.

This guide focuses on what you need to do to become a better negotiator. You will learn about how to negotiate with people and how to get better connections with others. Part of this includes knowing how to figure out what others need in any discussion. As you use the points in this guide, you will find that it is easy to figure out what people want out of any efforts you wish to work with.

Your work in negotiating with people will be very easy to manage when you use the points in this guide. As you follow the instructions listed here, you will see that it is not hard to find ways to get things out of a strong negotiation if you put in a good effort into the process.

__Why You Need to Build Upon Your Negotiation Skills__

Talking with other people is only natural. You have to talk with people all the time to get where you want. After all, you cannot just get the most out of your life unless you get a bit of extra help from other people.

It is a necessity for you to know how to negotiate well with other people. Whether it is in your daily life or for business purposes, negotiation skills are critical to your success. The reasons why you have to improve your skills are vital.

Create a Sense of Understanding

As you work on your negotiation skills, you will start to understand the needs that people have.

You are not the only person who is trying to get something beneficial out of work.

There is always a second side to a discussion. You have to respect how that other side operates. As you learn how to negotiate, you will start to understand what people are thinking and what motivates them.

As you begin to understand what someone wants, you will undoubtedly give that other entity the support it needs. You will show that you respect the needs someone has. This improves your chances of having a better overall negotiation with someone.

This is useful if your endgame is to establish a long-term relationship. Knowing how other people tick and behave gives you more control over the experience you have with someone.

Be Fair

Fairness is important in any situation. You might want to get somewhere but you have to respect the needs that others have.

When you negotiate with others, you are fair and under control. You are showing someone that you honor the needs that the person holds.

As you are fair, you show a sense of concern for other people. This gives you a better chance at being positive and helpful.

Be to Everyone's Benefit

The main goal of a negotiation is to help everyone with achieving what they are looking for. It focuses on you looking out for more than just yourself. It also requires you to show that you care about the needs that others in a situation have.

Even when you try to make the negotiation fit in line with your specific needs over everyone else's, you must still show that there is something in a negotiation for everyone. As you support the needs that others hold, it becomes easier for a conversation to move forward and stay strong.

Even if you are trying to compete with someone, you have to do something that gives the other side the impression that something good has happened. Whether it means acquiring something one needs or just keeping a bad issue from becoming worse, you have to give something positive to the other party.

Improve Your Bottom Line

Negotiations help you to keep your bottom line in check. As you work towards getting people together, you will find that it is not hard to get what you need. It all comes as you show what you want to do for someone and that you are ready to offer help or support in some way.

The general goal of a negotiation is to get the best possible deal on your end while satisfying the needs that someone else has. As you build upon your skills, you will understand everything you should do to improve your efforts while also avoiding the pitfalls that come with unfair discussions.

Build Confidence

Many people struggle in the workplace because they do not feel confident. They are uncertain as to what they can do when trying to talk with other people.

You have to feel comfortable with yourself and ready for anything if you wish to go somewhere with your negotiations. As you become confident, it becomes easier for you to deal with other people. You will feel ready to take on anyone without feeling worried about what might come about over time.

By working with negotiations, you start to understand yourself a little more. You begin to feel confident with your work and what you are doing in general. This gives you the extra boost you need to complete your work and support others.

Be Respected

People who do well with others in the workplace or any other environment are always respected by others. Those who are strong and ready to take on any challenge are more likely than others to be admired.

You will have a much easier time negotiating things with others when you have the skills needed for doing this. This all comes as people will have more respect for you. They would be more likely to concede some things to you.

Great skills also improve upon your reputation. People will see you as being a better person to do business with. The chances of you getting more long-term deals and agreements with people or at least extended relationships will increase.

All of these points prove just how essential negotiation skills truly are. Look at what you are doing for your efforts, and you will see that you can indeed go far if you just think about how well your negotiation plans can work in any situation.

Commonly Used Negotiation Styles

As you start working with people at the negotiation table, you will see that everyone has their objectives. What one person wants out of a deal is different from what you wish.

It is with this that you have to think about how you will negotiate with people. You must look into what you are doing when talking with others and showing that you care about the needs they have.

You will notice when negotiating with people that there are five styles you could work with. Each format focuses on two things:

1. What benefits do people get in the end?

2. Are people going to lose anything?

These five styles focus extensively on your wants and needs and those of the other party. We need to look at what makes each of these differences.

Compromise

We all want what is right for us but sometimes we have to make sacrifices to make it all work. This is where a compromise takes place.

In this style, both sides win some and lose some. It is all about the two sides willing to sacrifice a few things to get to the goals they really want.

This works in the event that there is a sense of concern between two parties. In this, both sides have their own specific goals that they want to attain. The two have to do something to make it easier for each of them to get somewhere.

People will discuss in a compromise what they have to give up to win. Each people aim to find an agreement that they can live with.

It is easier for such a strategy to work when you have a good relationship with the other party. You would have a smooth conversation with someone at this point without being judgmental or otherwise difficult to bear with.

More importantly, both sides can go away feeling as though they have won. While it is true that both sides will not get everything they want, they can at least go out knowing that they have gained something positive.

Think of the compromise strategy as one where you are splitting the benefits down the middle. This is not necessarily a truly fair deal among all sides as you feel you could have done better. Then again, the other party will feel the same way.

In short, a compromise is all about just finding a way for both sides to feel comfortable. It is not always perfect but it might be a necessity if there are substantial differences between you and the other party.

Collaborate

A great negotiation can bring two people to side with each other in many ways. It is about both sides recognizing that something positive can come about in a relationship. Specifically, the two will wish to work together with the same goals in mind.

Collaborations involve both sides winning in the process. There is a way for both people to find how they can get what they want without having to go through any disputes or issues.

The collaborative process focuses on problem-solving. You and the other party would look at what is happening at a given time and then figure out a way to resolve an issue. The goal is to figure out what each side values in a given situation.

The end result involves getting all sides to stick with the same endgame. This might involve both people sticking with certain ideas for success.

As the brainstorming session moves along, you and the other party figure out great ideas for resolving issues. Every solution ties into the final result you wish to attain.

The collaborative process requires you to be more assertive. You must express your needs for any situation.

Even so, you would still have to hear the needs that the other team has. You would adjust your plans to where your demands can accommodate those of the other party. Finding solutions for both sides to grow well is always great to think about.

This works best in cases where you are trying to establish a long-term relationship with someone. It also works well in cases where you are focused on a short-term project. You would have to look at how well the project is run.

Accommodate

It is not easy to enter a discussion where you are trying to just keep a good relationship going. You might have to think about what you would give to make sure people are happy even if you have to give up something.

You want to ensure that a long-term relationship is possible with someone. But to make it work, you have to bend over backwards to give someone the assets or solutions that entity needs.

When you accommodate someone, you are sacrificing some things that you want so that the other side can win. This is to get someone to be on your side. It happens when you want to do something for another person to establish a better relationship.

An accommodating plan will result in giving concessions to the other party. In some cases, you are willing to keep your end of the deal down so the other person ends up benefiting the most.

The most important part of accommodating someone's needs can lead to neglecting your own needs. You have to look beyond yourself and think about how someone else could benefit in some way. It is not always easy to do this but it is critical if you wish to move forward.

This is best when you are dealing with long-term relationships. It is also useful if the short term needs you have are not all that important.

Besides, you can always benefit from more good things coming from your negotiation partner later on. When you are generous, your new partner will feel the same way towards you. That person will want to give back when you do have trouble or special needs down the road. As a result, you are getting more support from another person.

Compete

Do you have a need for something right now? You might need help from other people to make it work. But sometimes it is not easy to convince them that you need help. You might have to put in some assertive moves just to get what you want in this case.

Those who want to move forward and dominate other people often stick with a competitive style of negotiation. In this style, you win something while the other party loses. This is not always easy but it happens when you want something and you know the other party in question is weak.

This works as people try to attain their goals regardless of the impacts that come about onto other people. If anything, a person who competes sees negotiation as a win or lose situation.

A competition is not about solving a problem. It is rather about trying to get a leg up on everyone else.

This is a form of negotiation that is not used very often because it often involves aggressive actions. People often attack or threaten others when they compete. Aggressive behaviors are critical to trying to move forward as you contend.

Competitive negotiations often highlight the worst case scenario. You discuss what could happen if a person does not stick with the offer you are presenting. While the offer might hurt in the short term, not acting upon it could be even more dangerous months or years down the road.

The competitive negotiation style is used in cases where long-term relationships are not important but the short term goals are.

This strategy could work if you establish a strong sense of rapport while also keeping yourself from sounding hostile. You must be calm and able to encourage someone without being too hard to manage.

Avoid

The last thing anyone wants to bear within a negotiation is a situation where all people are going to lose. Whether it entails economic troubles, natural disasters or outside competition that is far too strong, there are always problems that could get in the way of one's work. It is with this that the avoid style is to be considered.

The avoid style of negotiation is the last one that anyone would want to get into. This results in a lose-lose situation. Both sides have to give things up. Each party is not going to get much out of the deal. But in the end, it is all about the two sides finding a way to agree with one another and to keep a bad situation from being worse. Whether it includes outside competition or forces that are just beyond one's control, the avoid style is a necessity to understand.

There are times when a situation has to be resolved as soon as possible regardless of the results. It might include an issue where something terrible has come about and the risk is dangerous. More importantly, you would need to try and manage an argument so things do not get to be more of a threat.

The negotiation style is often where people step around issues or try to postpone them. In other cases, it involves getting a certain issue out of the way before it can persist any further.

This is made for just trying to preserve a relationship. It is also for cases where short-term issues are not all that important for people at a given time.

So with that in mind, here is a summary of the five:

Negotiation Style	Your Side	The Other Person's Side
Compromise	You win and lose	They win and lose
Collaborate	You win	They win
Accommodate	You give up things to the other party	They get the benefit
Compete	You dominate the other party	They struggle against you
Avoid	You lose something	They lose something

All five of these negotiation styles are distinct from one another over what results come out of each. Look at how well you are planning a negotiation and see that you produce a setup that is easy to follow and live with.

Who Uses What?

As you plan your negotiations, you must look at the styles that people are using at a given time. Review your own individual style that you naturally stick with and compare it with whatever your partner is using.

Think about how aggressive you might be or if you are focusing more on a more cautious approach. Look at what the other person in the negotiation is doing as well.

Get a closer look at the situation the other party is in. Is that party struggling financially? Are there obstacles that their team are bearing with right now? Is that team trying to surpass you in the economic climate?

More importantly, look at these two keys:

1. Think about how important to negotiation session is between you and the other party. Review the situation you want to resolve and if it is appropriate for you to take care of.

2. Understand the relationship you have with the other partner. A tougher approach could work if you do not plan on having an extended relationship with someone. Meanwhile, a lighter or more conciliatory method may work if you want to keep your connection lasting long.

Be ready for anything that could happen with all of these negotiation styles. You might be surprised when you look at the approach of the person you are negotiating with.

Planning a Negotiation Session

As you get ready to negotiate with someone, you have to look at how you can get the most out of your work. You must plan your work carefully, so it is easier for your session to operate well. Let us look at what you can do before you start negotiating with someone.

Determine Your Worth

Look at what you are trying to offer to someone. Whether it includes resources, concessions or services, you must look at what you would give to someone before negotiating.

You will have to give something to the other party in your negotiation. Look at how much your assets are worth. It might involve certain skills you have to offer or tangible goods that are needed for finishing certain tasks or making life easier.

Consider if your work or goods are valuable or rare. Maybe you might get away with a little more power if you have something of strong value.

Look at how you can be worthwhile to other people. You must find a way to make yourself more valuable and more appealing. You should figure out what gives you the edge in the discussion. Maybe you have assets that no one else has or you are easier to contact.

It is better to ask for more things from someone than it is to beg. When you know your value, you have more control over your discussion. You know what makes your work outstanding. You especially know how to make that effort attractive and useful to another party.

The most important thing is to show that what you have to offer has a strong value attached to it. Show that people will benefit from what you have.

Express Your Need

You must explain the need that you have with someone. Specifically, you need something another person has.

That need could be for anything. You might have a demand for a particular asset to keep a business afloat. Perhaps you need the services of someone to simplify how your business runs or to fill in gaps in existing processes.

When you explain your need, the smallest issues or concerns will be more viable and interesting to someone. Be willing to discuss what you want and that you are the right person for whatever it is you are asking for. Show that everything you wish to discuss has some special meaning to it and that you are not willing to sacrifice just anything.

Figure Out a Break-even Point

Eventually, your negotiation will reach a deadlock. You will have limits as to what you could do. You might not have the money or assets to give away. Perhaps you cannot sacrifice certain wants without putting your future work in jeopardy.

Think about a good break-even point that you could follow. This is to create a limit as to what you are willing to take.

The break-even point is the lowest benefit you will take in the negotiation. It is a point where you will receive something of value, but it will not be as much as you might wish. Think of it as a worst case scenario.

Figure out how low you can afford to go before planning your negotiations. Look at what you can do with them before anything difficult takes place in the discussion.

Plan Your Proposals

Every negotiation session has its series of proposals. You ask for something and in return, you give back. The transaction plan you hold is the basis of the negotiations.

There are several tips to use when planning a proposal:

- Be realistic at all times. Do not be overly lofty or hard as people can tell when you are aiming far too high.

- Ask for more than what you might expect to get at the start. Again, do not go overboard in whatever you wish to do.

- Figure out the break-even point that you are willing to stick with. You will learn more about this later in this guide.

- Recognize that the other party will be impacted in some way. Show in your proposal how your offer will benefit that group.

Use all of these points to get your negotiation session up and running the right way. You must plan your session to the point where it is not hard to talk with someone. It is also to show that what you have is appealing and viable for someone's demands.

How to Establish Rapport with Someone Quickly

Have you ever noticed cases where two business groups can get along with one another? The two CEOs seem to hit it off with each other and aren't argumentative or rough on each other. They know what each other wants.

A case of two CEOS getting along quite well is an example of having a reliable rapport. People who have such rapport know what each other want and are trustworthy.

One part of getting a negotiation session to go well can lead to having a strong rapport with whoever it is you are doing business with. You have to express that you care about the needs that someone has.

But what is rapport in particular?

Rapport entails the ability to establish a positive relationship with someone. It is all about showing that you care about the needs that another person has.

Rapport is all about several keys:

- Showing that you are easy for someone to trust
- Having a sense of positivity
- Establishing the feeling that what you want to do will be to everyone's benefit regardless of the result
- Showing a consistent sense of communication where all people involved have a shared sense of understanding

It can take a good deal of time for you to establish a great rapport with someone. But by using a few strategies, it will be easier for you to get that rapport going as soon as possible. The endgame is about expressing specific desires to help.

Have a Good Appearance

Sometimes a first impression makes all the difference. A person who does not dress well for the occasion or is unprofessional in behavior is hard to trust. You have to start your conversation with someone by establishing a good appearance and demeanor that is professional and strong.

Be prompt and ready to meet with someone during a negotiation session. Prepare a professional and comfortable appearance so you can show to someone that you care about the needs someone holds.

A good idea is to dress a little better than who you will be talking to. Do not overdress though or else you will make yourself feel as though you are better than that person. Just dress slightly nicer and it will be easier for you to have a look that you want to get out of your meeting.

Stand up straight and talk in a confident and vocal manner. Be clear in your words. Do not look like you are worried about your appearance either. Getting that look down right before you start the negotiation shows that you have put in all the effort you can into your work and that you are ready to talk with someone.

Be Comfortable

One way how you could wreck the rapport you are trying to develop would be if you were to imply that you were uncomfortable. Those who feel stressed out or worried are less likely to succeed in whatever they are doing. Those people are often nervous and do not show a single bit of confidence in their work.

Take a look at how your body is moving during the negotiation. Are you shaking around while trying to find a comfortable physical position to be in? Are you too busy thinking about stuff that could happen to the point where you cannot actually concentrate on what someone is saying?

You need to smile and relax when talking with someone. Show that you are calm and that you are not uncomfortable with whatever is happening. You might be amazed at how well a good sense of communication can make you go forward if you are just careful enough with your plans.

Do not feel stressed out or worried when you are talking. Be prepared to get into a relaxed position where you will not feel stressed or worried about what is happening where you are.

Keep your head up and show a good posture all the way around. Let the other party see that you are not afraid.

Show that you are not thinking about other stuff. Be comfortable in the place you are in and you will display that you are focused on what is happening right now. Such an action proves that you are firm on getting the negotiations done right away and that you're not going to wait for any longer to get what you want out of a conversation.

Listen To the Other Person

Always pay attention to whatever the other person in the conversation has to say. Do not ignore whatever it is the other person wants to tell you. You do not want to get into a situation where you do not sound professional.

As you listen to another person, you show that you have a vested interest in whatever someone wants to do. You are expressing that you care about the desires that person has and that you are not going to ignore that person's needs.

There are a few good things you can do when trying to listen to someone:

- Refrain from being distracted by other things. Avoid looking at your phone or other things that are moving or are rather bright. Try and get rid of such issues before you start listening to someone just to ensure you have a better chance of hearing whatever someone wants to say.

- Take a moment or two before you start listening to someone. Give yourself a clear head without thinking too much about other stuff that is on your mind.

- Listen to the tone of the other person's voice. Hear what someone is trying to say and think about how you're going to respond to that person's demands.

Just listening to someone is always positive. People prefer it when they know that others are hearing what they have to say. No one ever wants to feel ignored or disrespected.

After all, you might have a desire to keep a good relationship up and running with someone. You do not want to bear with problems where it is hard for you to interact with someone.

Mirror the Other Person

Mirroring the other person in the discussion is always good to do. Mirroring means you are utilizing the same emotions and attitudes as the other in the party.

To some, this sounds like trying to duplicate the same activities that the other person does. It could be tough to do but mirroring is an important life skill.

People like to be around others when they act similarly. They prefer it when their natural behaviors are confirmed by others to be normal in some way. It disarms any pressure in the room.

More importantly, the tone of your voice and your body language speak more than the actual words you say. Mirroring the tone and body language of the other person improves your chances at having a great conversation with someone.

To mirror another person, you have to follow a few strategies:

- See how the other person's body language works. Look at the posture that person has and the expressions someone makes. Try to mirror that person in many ways. For instance, if a person wipes one's brow off with one's left hand then you could do the same for yourself with your right hand so long as you are not doing it too soon or you are being overly dramatic in the process.

- Use the same attitude in your voice as what the other person is doing. Speak with a lighter tone if the other person is doing the same. Do not adopt a different tone or else you might project yourself as being too weak or strong depending on the variance.

- Speak with the same kinds of words that the other person uses. Do not stick with words that are too weak in comparison with the others. Avoid sounding overly smart or verbose or else the other party might feel insulted.

No matter what you do, keep all your changes as gentle and subtle as possible. Do not exaggerate or act too rough. You do not want to act like you know everything or that people might feel weak in comparison with you.

Create a Shared Experience

It is true that being unique is always important. But in a negotiation there comes a time when being unique is not good enough. You have to get everyone on the same boat in such a situation. Everyone needs to share their values and opinions in a way where no one will feel isolated or left out of the process.

Everyone in a room will feel better about a certain situation when they feel as though the experiences they are in are the same. Look at the needs that a person has for speaking and see how you can accommodate those concerns.

Discuss problems or concerns that you might have with someone. See that you can get the same understanding. As this happens, a shared experience develops as all people are of the same mindset. They have a good idea of what everyone wants.

The shared experience especially gets people involved on all fronts. Everyone is likely to feel ready for a good discussion without being rough or otherwise hard to understand.

Establish Common Ground

It is always easier to talk with someone when you can share something. When you share something with another person, you prepare common ground.

Allow the conversation to start with you and the other person talking about yourselves. Share points of what you like doing or your interests. Explain what your goals for the future might be.

Anything that invites conversation or possibly some form of comparison is always welcome.

Be open-ended when asking questions. Let the other person think about one's answer to a question that comes about. Do not be too restrictive or else the other person will feel uncomfortable or worried about whatever is being discussed.

Stay genuine when trying to establish common ground. Do not be overbearing or rough or you would struggle to keep everyone comfortable.

Is Humor Appropriate?

On a related note, you could also use humor to establish rapport. Humor is a universal language that can prepare the common ground with anyone quite well.

You have the option to crack a joke or two and lighten the mood if you can think of something. But if you're going to make it work, you have to think about the situation you are in.

- Do not try to make light of anything if the situation at hand is too rough. This includes a case where the stakes are very high or the pressure involved is extreme.

- Watch for how certain remarks could be interpreted by others in many ways. Do not bother saying something if you think it could be misconstrued by someone in any manner.

- Sarcasm can be fun if used well but in most cases, it is too difficult to manage. Avoid sarcasm if possible just to be safe.

Humor makes anyone feel better and keeps a serious situation from being too stressful or hard. Just watch for how you use it.

Be Transparent

Transparency is important for establishing rapport. This refers to how open and direct you are with someone.

When you are transparent, it becomes easier for you to show to someone that you understand what that person wants. You will be direct with others and willing to express to people what you want to get out of a conversation.

People are more likely to enjoy you when you are open. They do not like people to try to dance around issues or try to change their opinions just to fit in with someone.

Think about what might happen when you are talking with someone and that person is hiding things from you. Would you trust that person? Anyone who is secretive or quiet about the subject is not being transparent. That person might actually be too rough or hard to bear with.

Although it is important to do so, it might be a challenge to be transparent at times. You might think more about just saying things that make someone feel comfortable. Instead of doing this, just think about how good things can come about in a conversation without being rough or hard on someone.

Establishing rapport does not have to be tough to do. Look at what you are doing as you try to produce this as you need to show that you care about someone. Make everything work right, and you will notice that it is not overly hard to make a negotiation session work well.

How to Read People

Getting a good sense of rapport is easy to do when you understand the needs that someone has. But to get to those needs, you have to know how to read someone. Several strategies must work so you can identify the needs that someone holds.

Combine Many Gestures and Actions

You cannot judge a person just by one gesture or action. Look at all the things that someone is doing at a given time. Review how individual gestures combine after a while.

For instance, you might notice that a person keeps clearing one's throat and wiping one's brow. After a while, that person might be shaking one's knees.

Sometimes these are knee-jerk reactions that people do not always have full control over. They happen without a person noticing them. Such actions might seem innocent at the start but after a while, they could reveal some worries that people might have while in the negotiation process.

Look at how long some of these physical gestures or actions might go along for. For some people, it only takes a few moments for those physical issues to go away. In other cases, those problems might persist during the entire negotiation session. These problems develop as someone is unable to figure out ways to keep one's mind and body under control.

Be aware of how someone is responding to what you are saying. See that the things someone is doing are easy to figure out and that you have a clear idea of what someone is thinking or feeling.

Who Has a Strong Voice?

The next point on how to read people involves situations where you are dealing with more than one person. There is always that one person in the group that seems to have the most vocal tone or attitude. That person might be someone who is not afraid to share one's opinions or attitudes about whatever is happening at a given time.

The most confident people in the room are the ones that want to speak. They talk more often and feel upbeat when doing so. They are not necessarily loud but they do have voices that carry well.

Figure out who has the strongest voice and establish rapport with that person. Anyone who is willing to get out there and move forward will be easier to get in touch with during the negotiation process.

Do not assume that the person with the highest seniority or leadership role is always the one that has the most power. Sometimes a lower-level person might have a better pull over the situation. That person has a better idea of what is going on and could ask more questions or resolve situations quickly.

Review the Context

One problem people have when they try to read others is when they do not bother with context. There is always some meaning involved when getting in touch with someone.

For instance, a person might have one's arms crossed. This might look as though the person is reserved or closed to ideas. But in reality, that figure might be chilled as the air conditioner is running too hard. That person might not have any armrests on one's chair either, thus forcing that person to keep one's arms crossed.

Maybe someone is dealing with emotional or personal pressures that are keeping that person from thinking clearly. The stresses someone goes through in daily life could add up over time and make things harder for people to bear with.

Whatever the case is, review what is behind a person's behavior and attitude. You might find that the person in question is acting in a certain way because of particular problems that have built up over time and have become difficult to maintain or resolve in some way.

Review Baseline Behaviors

The last tip is to look at the baseline behaviors that someone exhibits. Every person acts differently from one another. Some are physically energetic while others are a little more laid back.

Look at how someone normally acts and see if there are any significant deviations from what one is doing at a given time. Consider the baseline of whoever you are acting with and see if there are any significant changes in the ways in which they are behaving.

Reading people is easy to do when you look at how they behave and what makes them distinctive. Look at how you can read people and see what you can get out of them so you can take more out of a conversation.

How to Identify the Needs of Your Counterpart

Part of the negotiation process can include understanding what the other person in the discussion feels. You have to look at what someone thinks about a certain situation if you want it to move forward without any hassles.

Don't Think About Your Needs

The general goal of a negotiation is to get something that benefits you or at least keeps problems from being worse. But what about the other person in the discussion? You cannot ignore that person in the least.

Keep your mind clear when looking at the needs that your counterpart has. Avoid thinking about what you want for a moment. Listen carefully to the other person and let your mind focus on what they are saying.

Thinking too much about your needs could cloud your judgment. You do not want to think for too long about something of value to you. Instead, think more about your demands.

Be prepared to look at what your counterpart is thinking when negotiating with that person. Be ready to do anything you can to see what someone is demanding or requiring.

If anything, you might change your goals for the negotiation once you see things in a new light. Looking at what someone is asking for and acknowledging that need is always vital for your success when talking with someone.

Look at Someone's Situation

Every person in a negotiation session has their own circumstances. These points often entail issues like financial concerns, resources or even skills. The personal issues that someone is bearing with could be a concern too.

Look at what someone is bearing with at a given time. The context surrounding what someone is going through is important to review as it relates to what could be happening that is keeping someone from being able to do things in a particular way.

Review the long-term efforts that your negotiation partner has in mind. You might discover that certain concepts are easier to follow when used well enough.

Be Direct When Talking

This point focuses less on identifying needs and more on how you are going to get around to finding those needs. As you talk with someone, you have to be very direct and specific with someone. Be willing to talk with someone about the needs that person holds.

As you stay open and direct, you will show that you are willing to be open. You are showing that you care about what someone is saying. By doing this, it becomes easier for you to make the most out of the conversation you wish to have.

Understanding another person's point of view and what that person needs is always critical to your negotiation skills. Look at how well your efforts are going about when you are helping someone during the negotiation process. Look at what you can do when figuring out the needs that someone has so it becomes easier for you to get more out of a negotiation plan.

The Big Open

After you establish a sense of rapport and understanding with your negotiation partner, you are ready to get to work. You are ready to talk about what you want, what the other party wants and how to get somewhere in the middle.

The big open is the first offer you make. It is not always the best offer. That deal is actually one that benefits you the most because you are starting out at a point that is more beneficial to you above others.

The opening offers in your negotiation session should be reviewed carefully. You will have to establish a good strategy for starting things off.

Remember, the negotiation will move from the first thing you offer to the final deal that people could agree upon. Get ready for the start and you will find it is not hard to get the most out of your work if used well.

Be High At the Start

Begin your negotiation by asking for something high but remember to be realistic. You probably will not get the higher deal but it never hurts to try. Besides, you might get it if you are lucky.

Ask for something well above whatever you are demanding. Think about what someone could realistically offer you and then set up a plan.

This shows that you highly value yourself and that you have an honest desire to do something great. More importantly, you show that you want to do something special and that you are determined to get it.

Do not go low at the beginning. A poor low-value offer not only shows that you are weak but also that you are not all that interested in the negotiation. The other party might even be insulted by your lack of effort, thus breaking off negotiations. Even worse, that person might try and take advantage of you and give you much less than what you are asking for.

Staying strong in the negotiation involves more than just being powerful even when things are not going your way. It also involves being ready for anything that could come about regardless of the situation at hand.

Offer Your Background

Your negotiation partner will be likely to ask you what you are thinking about and what makes you so different from other people. You must share your background with someone to explain what makes your ideas or concepts so intriguing.

Your background should include points like:

- Your experience
- What you value
- Your desires
- How far you are willing to go in the discussion

Showing your background gives the audience an idea of what makes your work so inviting. You are showing that you are ready for the conversation and that you really want to make something work out.

Listen to What the Other Parties Want

As you start the negotiation, pay close attention to what the other people in the discussion want to hear. Listen to what they have to say and that you are working alongside them to find solutions that they can all agree with.

Listening to people shows that you fully accept what they are asking for. It reinforces the rapport you built up at the start and expresses the strong value you have for helping others. Be certain you hear other people out and give them the assistance they require in any situation that may come about.

__Managing Manipulation__

There are often times when the person you are trying to negotiate with is aiming to manipulate the conversation or the situation at hand. This works in that someone is clearly going to try and alter the situation to one's favor. It is all about creating an unfair deal in the end.

Manipulation often occurs when someone tries to alter the outcome. With that in mind, you have to look at what you are doing when communicating with someone. You must see what you can do when getting the most out of your negotiation so it is not all that hard for you to get the most out of your efforts.

Watch for Pressure

Someone you are speaking to might try to add a significant amount of pressure to the situation you are in. There are two forms of pressure that someone might force on to you:

1. Competition gets in the way. The other party brings others who are far outside of the negotiation into the fold. Someone might say that you are contending with others and that you have to make concessions or changes to be favored. This is all about making yourself look better than others but in most cases, it often involves lowering your standards just so you can get a deal.

2. Deadlines frequently go in your work when someone tries adding pressure into the mix. These are added to create pressure to make you put in a decision right now.

Such problems make weak people want to decide on things right now. They are afraid of what could happen and would rather do something immediately rather than try and negotiate to keep the issue from being one-sided.

These problems can be alleviated if you ask questions to the other person. Ask about why certain deadlines exist and if they are all that necessary. Figure out where any deadlines come from and if there are possible extensions available. Do not let go of your demands because someone is forcing you into acting in a brief period.

Ask about the competition that you are facing. What does someone want to do when trying to change a narrative? Look at what is causing the competition to heat up and see if it is worthwhile or even threatening to you in some way.

There often is a good reason why someone is trying to force a certain amount of pressure onto you. Look at what someone is trying to say or do and think about what can be done to resolve the pressure that is coming about.

Delaying

Some negotiators try to delay the process. They often say that they have a limited amount of control in a situation and need an extra bit of time to find a resolution.

Others might say they are missing certain people. They need that one last person to come over to take care of a discussion or dispute.

Delay tactics are used by people to gain an extra bit of time. There is the belief that delaying makes it easier for someone to figure out ways to make the discussion a little more one-sided.

More importantly, people delay things because they feel what they have right now is too weak. They need an extra bit of time to bolster their arguments. Delaying is a sign of someone being very weak and unwilling to make changes or support certain things in the argument that comes along.

When talking with another party, ask to speak with whoever is responsible for making certain decisions. Talk with those who make the final decisions in certain disputes or conversations. Ask if there is a way how certain problems can be resolved directly.

Moral Manipulation

The art of manipulation is all about changing someone's emotions. People are vulnerable to many appeals and the largest of those are often the most powerful and moral.

Think about the public service announcements you watch on television. Some use emotional appeals to encourage you to live in a certain way. They might tell you about the dangerous using drugs or what happens if you do not keep your home safe and protected from fires or other threats.

These often manipulate your emotions by explaining that engaging in certain behaviors will hurt you and the ones you love the most. There are several better ways for people to explain things that they feel are important but they still like to manipulate your emotions just to make you feel sorry.

Sometimes morality might get in the way of the conversation. A person would say that you have to use moral judgment in that you are not always going to get everything you want out of a discussion.

In this case, discuss what can be done with the best interests of you and the other party in mind. Ask about what would happen to the other party if something does not go in a particular way. You must look at the general motivation that someone holds as it might be the key to why someone is trying to manipulate you into taking in an answer.

The Good Guy-Bad Guy Approach

One of the most common approaches you might see in the media is the good guy-bad guy method. This is where one person is trying to be friendly and calm while the other is a little more aggressive and confrontational.

This strategy has been played out in the movies quite a bit. You might have seen movies where one tough cop is being angry and hostile towards someone. Meanwhile, another cop is being nice and friendly. People like to make fun of this trope all the time because of how outlandish and silly it can be. But there is a reason why this trope exists. It is a move that works when convincing people to take deals.

The bad guy in the situation is intimidating and rough. The moves the bad guy makes are all about trying to gain traction in a discussion.

The good guy then comes in and tries to be more reasonable. The good guy's moves might not always be in your favor or fair, but they appear as an alternative to what the bad guy is offering. It just looks better in comparison with what that second person is sending out.

This method of manipulation worries you as you aren't going to get anywhere if you just stick around and let the bad guy hassle you. But even so, it involves the best possible situation cheating your way out of something just because that person's ideas look and sound appealing.

Ask about the terms that the good guy presents in the discussion. See if they fit in with your goals. Do not be led astray by what that person says as that person might not be ready to give you a fair shot at something.

Blanketing

Have you ever heard people say stuff like "Everyone is doing it" or "Why would you want to miss out?" If so they have been experienced blanketing.

Blanketing is a generalization process. It is where someone says that everyone is doing something. A person might say that everyone in your sector is doing something like lowering prices, changing services and so forth.

It is a strategy used by people in advertisements today. You might see a commercial for some soft drink where the announcer says that everyone is trying out some new product. The message makes you feel left out because you have not tried something, thus making you want to run to your local store to buy that product regardless of its cost.

This form of intimidation is designed to make you act like everyone else. It is about trying to make you change your attitude or action based on something you might have seen.

Look at the standards within your industry or field of debate before entering a negotiation. Think about the business side of what you are doing and what others in your field are getting into. What you know might be different from what someone else claims to know about the situation you are in.

You might hear someone say that everyone is doing something. Ask who that "everyone" in particular is. Can the person you are talking to give you an honest answer? This could help disarm that person and force that someone to be a little more honest or direct with you.

Just because people say that something is appealing does not mean it is always worthwhile. Blanketing is a dirty strategy, but it can be avoided if you just think about why someone is telling you to do something.

The Association Tactic

The last form of pressure or intimidation that you could be subjected to is the association tactic. Someone might say that you remind that person of something else. That person might talk about past activities with someone similar to you or about what the situation at hand might be like.

This is not always worthwhile because someone might just be dropping names. It is all about trying to make you feel like someone else. The other party wants you to stick with the same concepts or ideas that one wants to follow.

Ask the other party about what that entity has done with someone that you are constantly being compared with. What does the other team see in some figure that is supposedly similar to you? Is it even possible for you to attain the same status?

When you review the association someone puts in, you begin to notice why someone acts in a certain way. The other person in the negotiation might think he or she is really powerful because that person is located so close to something.

In summary, it is easier for you to get a good result out of negotiations if you think about how people might try to manipulate you. Look at how people will try and change your mind or attitude about something. Be aware of what someone might be doing when trying to change your mind. You might be surprised at what someone could do when trying to change your mind or attitude about something.

The Use of Leverage

Part of your negotiation triggers someone to get a little closer to your side. It is often about getting what you want although it could also be to at least create a sense of understanding between two parties. Leverage is often needed to get there.

Leverage is something you must use when negotiating a deal with someone. It is the power you have to influence someone during the negotiation process. Your effort moves the needle in some way.

With leverage, you are showing that something is viable to another person. By showing this value, the other party will be ready to give you something in exchange for it. The things you have let you manage the conversation while naturally preparing a compromise.

Types of Leverage

To start working with leverage, you have to understand the individual forms you can use. Sometimes that leverage relates to what can be done to everyone's benefit. In other cases, you might hold something that could harm your negotiating partner unless you get things to go your way. The leverage style you hold must be used well and cautiously for your general success.

There are three particular types to work with as each of these stands out in its own way:

Positive Leverage

Positive leverage refers to your ability to provide someone with something of value. It is about satisfying the demands someone has.

For instance, you might say that you will give someone a beneficial item in exchange for something that is good for your end. It is a basic aspect of what you are offering as you are showcasing whatever good things it is you want to give to someone.

Negative Leverage

Negative leverage is where you are able to make someone else's situation worse unless that person agrees to your demands.

This is not necessarily going to bring about anything other than you having a stronger demand to be heard. The most common example of this comes from when someone is on strike. A party that is on strike will withhold itself services and will demand to have one's negotiations reviewed. This is negative as the striking entity is showing that it has the power to take away where it has to offer until certain demands come along.

This form should be used in cases where you do not have many other options to work with. Over time, you have to use this to show that you are serious about the issues you have and that you want them resolved right away.

Normative Leverage

Normative leverage necessitates vital social standards that might encourage people to agree upon something. With this, people look at what they feel are suitable and appropriate based on social norms.

This often warrants following through on some of the beliefs or demands that someone holds. You might be willing to cater to the religious standards that someone has or the budgetary limits that another party follows.

Get Information from Someone

Look at how the leverage you used is managed so you can get in touch with someone better. As you acquire more information, you will get to fully understand what someone is asking for.

You need to gather enough data on whatever someone wants or needs if you want to make it all work well. The leverage you use will help you learn a little more about anyone of interest to you. This, in turn, gives you an added amount of help in going somewhere in the discussion.

Always Be Credible

Regardless of the leverage you use, whatever you are offering should be credible and realistic. It should be something the other party can identify as being realistic and sensible. When you are fully credible, it becomes easier for the audience to understand what makes what you are offering so viable.

The leverage must be of a decent value to the other party. It should illustrate what makes an offer ideal and how you implement your work.

It must also clearly show what could happen if the other party does not accept what you are offering. You have to explain what could happen if that person does not stick with your plans.

Look at how your leverage is organized so you have extra control over your negotiation. Look at what you are saying to people and show that your ideas are appealing and useful.

__The Closer__

As you wind your way through the negotiation process, you will eventually reach what might be the end. This is where the closer comes into play.

The closer is a final discussion of offers you might make as you come close to the end. This works when you are almost able to complete a deal, but you just need an extra push when trying to get what you want.

This is not always the last thing that happens. It is simply a means of getting people near the end so they can find a way to resolve an issue or get the negotiation session to come to a proper finish.

Persuasion Is Key

As you work on getting a closer ready, think about how you would go forward with your demands. Show that you are ready to make a final deal and that you need to do a few things to make it all work in the end.

Persuade the other party about what makes your offer viable and suitable. Explain to them how the offer is to their benefit and why it is sensible and easy to use.

Show that you understand the needs someone has. Explain to them how what you are promoting is great for the requirements one has and that you are ready to help that person based on their needs.

Avoid Being Too Direct On Your Needs

Never be overly direct when trying to tell someone what you want. You have to explain to your audience that you have good ideas in mind and that you are not afraid to make them work to your benefit.

Being too direct makes it harder for someone to take you seriously. The other side might think you are too needy or demanding.

Instead, discuss with your negotiation partner what makes the assets you are offering valuable and appealing. Explain that what you have to say is worthwhile and that you are serious about giving someone the help and support that one desires.

Stay Firm

Be firm with whatever you want to offer. Do not go below the break-even point that you set up earlier. Stay stubborn and the other party will see how serious you are about something. This should give that party the chance to tailor one's demands or offer to fit what you specifically want.

Not sticking with your requirements is a real sign of weakness. You cannot show people that you do not care all that much. You must instead show that you have a significant interest in what you want to work with. Stay determined and ready for whatever could happen.

Closing the negotiation is easy to do when you figure out how to make it all worthwhile. Be certain that you plan your closer right and that you do not back down. Sticking with such an effort could be vital to your success.

How to Secure a Pay Raise

Let's talk about one of the more common ways where people should negotiate. People often negotiate efforts to make more money at their jobs.

Many people negotiate with money in mind. They do what they can to show their value to someone and to explain why they are good candidates for big raises.

It is possible for you to secure a pay raise at your job? You have to negotiate well so you can get the most out of your employer.

Don't Be Afraid

Start your plans for negotiating well before you talk with someone. Do not fear your plans before you start talking. Many people are afraid to negotiate because they don't want to get in trouble. But the truth is that fear will not get you anywhere.

You have to be ready for anything that comes about in the discussion you hold. Do not be afraid about the bad things that might happen if you struggle.

Be Adamant

Do not think that what you have is good enough. The odds are you have a value to your employer that no one else could ever give. Being adamant about what you wish to do is important to see.

Showing that you care and that you do not want to stop working on something is a sign of strength. It shows the target audience that you are dead serious about what you are trying to offer to someone.

Discuss Your Value

Think about the work that you do and how important it is. What value do you give to your employer? Are the services you have to offer hard to duplicate or replace? Do you complete your work better than others?

Show that you have a significant value to your employer that cannot be easily replaced. This gives you the leverage needed for keeping the conversation going. It especially reminds your employer that what you are offering is valuable and essential.

The goal here is to explain that the quality of your work makes you irreplaceable. You have your special contributions to make in the situation. Express what makes you viable and critical to one's success.

Know How to React When Someone Says No

There is always a potential that your boss will reject your request for a larger pay rate. Do not feel let down if this happens. Instead, you have to know what to do to be considered for a raise in the future.

The most important thing to remember is that your employer is not going to think any less of you. The decision to not raise your salary is nothing more than just a basic business move. Perhaps your boss does not have the money to give you a better pay.

If anything, there is always the chance that you will still get a pay raise in the future. Sometimes a "no" is your employer saying that the person could give you more money later on, but at this juncture, it would not be possible for you to get a raise just yet.

Stick with whoever you are employed with, and the odds are you will get a pay raise after a while. When the business starts to grow, and its financial situation starts to improve, there is always the chance that you will get a raise. You might also have the option to ask for a raise then as the chances you have for a raise will increase.

Be careful when negotiating a pay raise. You will get more out of your employer if you look at how you the process works.

Quick Negotiation Strategies

Let's look at a few quick moves you can use when trying to negotiate a strong deal with someone. These ideas focus on special things that improve your chances for success. Each solution is also easy to implement.

Stay Consistent When Negotiating

Stick around as long as possible in your negotiation. Do not feel like you have to give an answer right away.

Those who stay during the negotiation are more powerful than others. They are determined to get what they want.

Anyone who takes many breaks and is impatient will not be likely to get what one wants during a negotiation session. People who are active and ready to talk about anything in a negotiation are much stronger and willing to do anything.

Do not assume that you can get a negotiation settled quickly. Think about some of the negotiations between businesses you hear about in the news. You might hear stories about discussions going all the way into the late hours of the night. Some people are willing to talk with one another for hours on end and will not stop until a connection runs.

Be ready to stick around for a while. Do not give up early. Be consistent regardless of how long the negotiation process lasts.

Silence Is Golden

Sometimes the best thing to say when getting your way is nothing at all. Being silent at the right times helps you get more out of what you want.

You will have to talk about what you want at the beginning. Showing your strength at the start is vital to your success. But after you introduce your work and explain what you want the most, you have to be a little muted and in control of what you wish to say.

Do not reply right away when someone makes an offer. Be quiet so the audience can see that you are thinking about it and that you are in deep consideration.

Your negotiating partner might end up feeling uncomfortable as you are silent. Do not worry about this. Rather, look at how the partner is forced into thinking about a new idea or strategy. Such a new move might be designed just to try and break the silence.

Let what you discussed earlier speak for itself. You will see that it is not hard to move forward in your discussions when you plan things right.

Giveaways Work When You Get Things

You may give things away to someone in the negotiation. But when doing so, you must have the ability to get something in return. Offer something special and then ask for a return of around the same value.

For instance, you might be trying to establish an agreement for exchanging certain items between businesses. You could say that you will give $10,000 to the other business to help it operate its regular expenses and to expand. But in return, you would ask for merchandise or goods totaling around $10,000 in value.

This does not necessarily sound like a true giveaway when all going into the situation. You are simply giving the other person something in exchange for another item at or close to the same value. But this shows that you are willing to give support and that you have a vested interest in whatever the other person is offering you.

Look At Future Concerns

Review things in the future that may come about and directly influence the negotiation. Think about how well certain ideas might work based on the future.

Look at what influences will work now and in the future. Talk with your audience about what they want in the long term and if the deal you wish to establish is viable for future needs. Remember that the short term is always important, but you should at least look at what could come about in the future.

Negotiation Case Studies

To understand what makes negotiation all the more important, it helps to look at a few case studies that show just how it works. These are examples of what goes on in a negotiation session as sides aim to keep problems from developing or being too hard to manage.

The United States and Syria

One good example of a negotiation came in 2013 when the United States and Syria had issues with one another. There were accusations that the Syrian government used chemical attacks on its people. This included one attack that killed nearly a thousand people. This was designed to suppress the opposition in the country.

The United States seriously considered launching a missile attack on the country. This would involve an attack on a military base or another target with the intention of weakening the country as a punishment for the attack.

However, there were concerns within the Syrian government that such an attack would cripple the nation's economy. It would also keep it from growing or thriving.

As a result, negotiations took place between the two countries. The United States held leverage in the discussion in that the country had more military power and was willing to use it against the Syrian government.

Discussions over what could be done to keep chemical attacks from occurring again were made.

In the end, a proper agreement was finalized. The American government agreed not to issue military action against Syria. In return, the Syrian government would destroy its chemical arms and end its plans for developing more of those weapons.

This is an example of an accommodating negotiation. Syria is accommodating the needs of the United States by ensuring it will not attack its people or use chemical weapons again. The moves were all to ensure that the country will not be attacked or threatened by the United States.

It is true that the United States and Syria have not necessarily had the best relationship over the years. But the negotiation at least helped keep some sense of peace in Syria as the government is looking to be more supportive of its people. Meanwhile, the United States has not dealt with any significant quarrels or issues with the Syrian government in recent time.

NHL Negotiations

The second case study to observe involves negotiations between the National Hockey League and its players' organization, the NHL Players Association. In 2004, the two sides were at a massive standoff over a collecting bargaining agreement. There were extreme divides between the two sides over how revenue was going to be shared between players and owners.

The deadlock between the two sides led to the prominent sports league canceling an entire season. In the summer of 2005, the two sides got together for negotiations.

The work between the players and owners is an example of an avoidance negotiation. That is, both parties are looking to avoid serious problems from developing.

The NHL had already suffered a massive black eye as the league's fans were being alienated while media partners and sponsors were backing out of supporting the league. More importantly, there were concerns that the NHL could end up canceling a second full season due to the labor dispute.

With these worries in mind, the owners and players got back together to negotiate a plan for managing salaries and revenue sharing. This all led to a new salary cap that would vary based on revenues plus the rights for players to become free agents at a younger age.

In the end, the two sides were not fully able to get every single thing that they wanted in the process. The owners did not get enough control of their players while the players had limits as to how much they could earn in a season. But it was all about avoiding future problems. This came as the threat of the work stoppage lasting even longer would result in more problems for the two sides in the future.

Thanks to the negotiation, the league has got back to playing games. Also, the league has grown in size and popularity with revenues, sponsorship deals and media contracts being worth more than ever before. Both sides were required to give up plenty of things just to make this happen.

Chicago Teacher Issues

In 2012, the city of Chicago was in dispute with the Chicago Teachers Union. The difficulties between both sides led to a ten-day strike where the teachers in one of the country's largest school districts did not show up for work.

Much of this came as the teachers were concerned about changes made by the newly elected mayor of Chicago. They felt that the mayor wanted to replace the public schools in the city with non-unionized schools. The city also adjusted laws relating to what teachers were allowed to strike for as teachers could only strike for salaries and nothing else.

The teachers and the city went into negotiations to figure out what could be done to keep problems from being worse. The city of Chicago agreed to give teachers rises every year while also extending the length of a school day.

Meanwhile, executives at the school system could continue to get raises, but they would be on par with what the teachers themselves are getting. The fairness established was a vital part of the discussion.

This case study is not only an example of the city accommodating the needs that teachers had but also an instance of how manipulative tactics do not work.

The city used the delay strategy to manipulate the teachers. Part of this lead to the city negotiating with individual schools while also increasing the threshold for approving a strike among teachers.

As the city tried to delay the negotiation, the teachers became more resilient and demanded more answers from the city. This led to the strike and eventually prompted further negotiations to take place.

The three case studies here are good examples of what makes negotiations so important. They can relate to not only resolving issues but also with understanding what should be done to keep the discussion under control. Whether it means keeping the damage to a minimum or simply asking for more control, it is vital for people to look at what they are doing.

Negotiating By Phone or Email

Many people negotiate in person. When the American and Syrian governments held their negotiations in 2013, they had key representatives meet with one another to discuss certain things to broker a sense of peace and control. Meanwhile, the National Hockey League's players and owners meet with one another many times to keep the damage to the league from being worse.

But while those two historic examples involve people meeting one another in person, there are often times when people might negotiate in other ways. The process used for negotiating with someone should be reviewed as sometimes the way how a message is delivered can make a difference.

On the Phone

When you negotiate over the phone, your voice comes through while no one can see your body language. All the details you wish to share will come through but not every aspect of your conversation will be noticed.

This form of negotiating may work in cases where you are trying to create a strong message. You could talk by phone when you are very direct in what you wish to say and that you want to keep distractions from getting in the way.

But even with that, just negotiating by voice can be a challenge. Attention and detail are vital.

There are a few things that should be done if you wish to negotiate with someone over the phone:

- Be prepared not only for what you wish to say but also for how you will respond. A phone negotiation is fast-paced as silence is often a sign of weakness. Being quick and ready to respond is a sign that you understand what the other party wants or is thinking and that you have answers for anything that might come along.

- Keep all your notes transcribed properly. You only have verbal information to work with. Write down your notes as they come along.

- Initiate the call if possible. Whoever starts the call has more power. As you dial up the person, you are bringing that figure into the fold. You are expressing your power with the potential for that strength to stay intact during the entire negotiation session.

- Allow for other people on the line to have time. Ask for others to get on the line to talk with you on occasion. Have just one idea come along at a time so the organization of the discussion is kept in check.

- Ask about anything your negotiation partner has to offer. Have that person be more descriptive about everything someone has. Anyone who is highly detailed when talking about things is easier to trust and support.

By Email

Negotiating with email gives you the opportunity to share more important pieces of data with someone. You have as much space as you want in your email to discuss certain points.

With an email, you could add charts or other attachments to your message. You could explain to the reader what you wish to share and that the general plans you put into your email negotiations should be reviewed. There are several things you can do to get your email discussions off and running:

- Explain your emotions about the situation at hand. Show that you have a human side. It is easy to do this when you write out your words and show how they mean something special to you.

- Add details to your discussion. Explain all the things you are trying to offer.

- Include multimedia to show more detail in your proposal. This is for cases where the data is very technical and specific.

- Solicit a response by introducing your own concerns or doubts. Explain any concerns you feel the other person might have or even worries you hold. Show the audience that you care about their needs and that you want feedback in your response.

- Express your confidence in the offer you are making.

- Do not assume that the meaning of every sentence being written is bad or serious. Just because a person writes something really serious in your email does not mean that it is as significant as you might think.

Look at what you can do when negotiating with someone by email or phone. These are both very different ways to get in touch with someone but can be useful if you think carefully about what is happening.

Negotiation Checklist

The final point to talk about in this guide involves knowing what you can do when negotiating with someone. This checklist includes information on everything you could do to get more out of your work.

Here is a look at what you should include when getting a negotiation session up and running:

Before

- Understand who you will be negotiating with. Look at that person's background.

- Figure out the format that you will use when negotiating. Determine a time and location.

- Review your leverage and what you can say to move the situation forward.

- Understand the long and short-term impacts of your negotiation. Figure out what each side has to lose or gain.

- Determine what you are willing to concede to your negotiation partner.

- Prepare a target for what you are willing to do.

- Review what the other person wants.

- Analyze the values of everything on the table. Some assets or other offerings might be more valuable than others.

- Figure out the lowest possible offer you are willing to stick with.

- See what items or concepts you have are expendable. Think about what you would give up just to make the discussion move forward.

During

- Be professional and courteous as you start.

- Get a clear mind and focus on what you want to get out of the negotiation. Think about the effects it has on you and your partner.

- Analyze what your discussion partner is doing. Whether they are using a negotiation strategy or question the image that person is projecting, evaluate carefully and see how you can use this to your advantage.

- Address the needs the other person has.

- Be flexible when figuring out what can be done.

- Show respect and care for the other person in the discussion. Do not ask as though you are superior in any manner.

At the End

- Prepare a detailed agreement regarding what the two sides are sticking with.

- Thank the other party for your time. Show courtesy even at the end.

- Do not get overly confident as the negotiation ends. Think about the issues the other person is bearing with.

- Confirm that both sides are going to be in a better standing at the end of the session. Whether it means one person being better off or another person limiting losses or other worries, think about how the two sides will respond.

Use the points in this checklist every time you get into a negotiation. You will understand more about what people need when you use the points listed here.

Conclusion

Getting in touch with someone to hammer out a deal is always important to do. You must know how to work with someone in a fair way while being sensible and easy to do business with.

This guide has shown you everything you need to do to make your negotiations work out properly. You should use the points listed here to get an idea of what you can get out of any negotiation plan without any problems.

As you get into a negotiation session, think about how it will run and what you can do to get all sides to feel confident and comfortable with whatever is being offered. Show that you care and that you have a good plan on hand for moving forward and making a discussion stand out and be viable.

Good luck with your efforts in negotiating with others. You will see when using the points in this guide that it is not all that hard for you to get more out of your efforts for supporting a strong and constructive talk.

Finally, if you enjoyed this book, please take the time to share your thoughts and post a review on Amazon. It would be greatly appreciated!

www.ingramcontent.com/pod-product-compliance
Lightning Source LLC
Chambersburg PA
CBHW070250230526
45470CB00002B/555